Dare TO be ME

Design by Andrea Kelly
Illustrations by Ana Martín Larrañaga

Library of Congress Cataloging-in-Publication Data available.

ISBN: 978-1-68555-747-8
Ebook ISBN: 978-1-68555-645-7
LCCN: 2023900404

Printed using Forest Stewardship Council certified stock
from sustainably managed forests.

Manufactured in China.

1 3 5 7 9 10 8 6 4 2

The Collective Book Studio®
Oakland, California
www.thecollectivebook.studio

DARE to be ME

Written by
Kaci Bolls &
NathanMeckel

THE
collective
BOOK STUDIO

Illustrated by
Ana Martín
Larrañaga

a PLAIN white Tee.

I wake up BRAVE,
and I DARE to be ME!

I sing to the sun and
Spin with the stereo,

filled up with JOY
like a big bowl of cereal.

It might scare me, but dare me—
watch me go LIVE IT.

In a sky full of pigeons,
I'm a PINK FLAMINGO flyin'.

For every basket of fries
covered in ketchup,

there's a tater tot like me
saying, "HEY MUSTARD. WASSUP?!"

I used to feel worried to just be MYSELF.

I couldn't blend in with EVERYONE else.

In a copycat costume, I TRIED TO BELONG.

But if sameness is right,
I DARE to be WRONG.

I'd rather stick out than shrink to FIT IN.

It's some kind of scary to have to audition for somebody else's PERFECTED position.

The SUN wouldn't dare
pretend it's the MOON.

So WHY would I try
and dare to be YOU?

If the shoe doesn't fit,
    there's NO need to fake it.

Wear your own pair,
be BOLD and go BRAVE it.

Salt can't be
PEPPER.

It's as simple as that—no minus, ALL plus.

It's a win-win world when we DARE to be US.

Spin with the stereo
and dance like a flamingo!
Scan now to hear the song
"Dare to Be Me."